WATER FROM THE ROCK

*Finding Grace
in Times of Grief*

Lyn M. Fraser

PAULIST PRESS
New York • Mahwah

Cover design by Moe Berman.
Cover photo by Fernando Rico.
Illustrations by Frank Sabatté, CSP.

Copyright © 1994 by Lyn M. Fraser

The royalties for this book are being shared with the Hospice of Brazos County, Bryan, Texas.

Library of Congress Cataloging-in-Publication Data

Fraser, Lyn M.
   Water from the rock : finding grace in times of grief / Lyn M. Fraser
      p.   cm.
   ISBN 0-8091-3504-3 (pbk.)
   1. Bible. O.T. Psalms—Meditations.   2. Grief—Religious aspects—Meditations.   I. Title.
BS1430.4.F73 1994   94-25003
242'.4—dc20   CIP

Published by Paulist Press
997 Macarthur Boulevard
Mahwah, New Jersey 07430

Printed and bound in the
United States of America

CONTENTS

FOR THE FAMILY, FRIENDS, AND CREATURES
WHO HAVE INSPIRED AND INFORMED THE
WRITING OF THIS BOOK.

Acknowledgments

With grateful appreciation I would like to acknowledge the many persons who have contributed to the writing and publication of this book.

The book would, literally, never have happened without the support and opportunities provided by the Hospice of Brazos Valley where I am a patient volunteer and facilitator of bereavement support groups. Dian Jones, Hospice Bereavement Coordinator, encouraged the writing from its inception. Several other Hospice professionals have been enormously helpful, and I would like to mention with special thanks John Foster, Executive Director, Anne Hazen, Patient Care Coordinator, and Rita Ewing, Volunteer Coordinator. By their actions and interactions, the entire staff of the Hospice Organization offers a daily and ongoing model for dealing in healthy ways with death and loss. And I am especially grateful for the rich experiences I have had with my Hospice families and my companions in bereavement support groups.

Many years ago, I made a covenant with a college friend, Julia Dorsey Loomis, now an Episcopal priest, to share a common spiritual discipline that included memorizing many of the psalms. The importance of the psalms in my daily life and the content of the personal reflections I have written have been greatly affected by that long-ago covenant.

Countless other friends have helped make this book

possible. In particular, I would like to thank Maureen Neal, who teaches writing at Texas A&M University; she has given loyal and caring support at every stage of the writing of this book, including editing the manuscript through several drafts. Patti Ljungdahl, whose husband was killed at mid-life in a tragic automobile accident, has shared lovingly and generously her journey through grief; and I greatly appreciate her comments on the manuscript during the writing process. Karen Hillier Woodfin, artist and teacher, encouraged the writing in its early stages. And I would like to express my loving thanks to the Rev. Jeffrey Schiffmayer and the entire parish community of St. Francis Episcopal Church.

Don Brophy and the staff of the Paulist Press have handled this project with extraordinary grace.

And this list would definitely not be complete without mentioning my household of creatures—Little Bit, Babe, R.T., and Piccadilly Circus—who have trampled, squashed, crumpled, scratched, and sat upon the pages of this book in all of its stages.

Finally, I would like to thank the members of my family. In particular, I want to express my loving appreciation to my daughter, Eleanor, who has been a major influence and source of support throughout my writing career. There were many times when I might not have continued without her unwavering and caring belief in my work.

Lyn Fraser
College Station, Texas
Spring 1994

LIVING THROUGH LOSS

Introduction

"How long must I bear pain in my soul, and have sorrow in my heart all day long?"

"Every night I flood my bed with tears. My eyes waste away because of grief."

"My heart is pierced within me."

"My friends and companions stand aloof from my affliction, and my neighbors stand far off."

"I am weary with crying; my throat is parched. I looked for comforters, but I found none. I am lowly and in pain."

"You keep my eyelids from closing. My soul refuses to be comforted."

"My strength fails because of my misery."

"I am too wasted to eat my bread. I lie awake; I am like a lonely bird on the housetop."

These comments reflect common feelings, questions, and experiences of those who are suffering the pain of grieving. We do not know who the grieving individuals are, however, because the expressions were recorded by Old Testament psalmists who wrote more than two thousand years ago.

When we lose someone or something important, we grieve. Grief is a normal response to loss. We grieve when someone we love dies: our spouse, our child, our parent, our relative, our friend, our mentor. And grief is not just related to the death of a loved one; the grieving process is essential for working through any important loss, whatever its source. We grieve the loss of relationships, homes, and jobs. We grieve the loss of a family unit from divorce. We grieve the loss of our youth. We grieve the loss of pets. We grieve the loss of our capacity to reproduce. We grieve when children leave home. Our grief in some way honors and reflects the quality of the relationship or experience that we have lost.

Grieving enables us to restore balance, to reclaim our circumstances, and to find new meaning in our lives after suffering a loss. Although it is a healthy and healing process, no two people grieve alike; it is uniquely *our* way of dealing with a personal loss, fully known only to us. And grieving is hard work. No one can do it for us, there is no right or wrong way to grieve, and there is no prescribed length of time for completing grief work.

As I have searched for support and resources in times of loss, my own and others', I return again and again to the psalms. There have been times when it has seemed to me that no one truly understood how I felt except the psalmists who wrote all those centuries ago.

Whether we read them as prayers, poetry, or meditations, the psalms probe the depths of our hearts and souls. They express the human condition honestly and directly, just where we are. Through the psalms, we find the intensity and range of feelings associated with loss—rage, shock, horror, anger, fear, guilt, despair, pain, and sorrow *as well as* grace, hope, assurance, courage, and comfort. The psalmists write of darkness and light, paradoxes, ambivalence, acceptance, and assurance. The psalms allow us to be fully ourselves in the presence of God, wherever we are in our own journey.

Reflections on the Psalms

This book contains my personal reflections on the psalms as I have worked through the grieving process—in my own life, with others in my community, and within the Hospice organization as a patient volunteer and bereavement support group facilitator. As a person who relies on daily scriptural meditations as part of my own spiritual journey, the psalms are an integral part of my everyday life. For me, the psalms provide a universal language of spirituality. They convey a message of compassion, support, and hope while acknowledging the intense pain that accompanies serious loss. And the psalms provide space for the inner growth that is essential to grief and recovery.

These reflections cover many of the emotions, activities, experiences, needs, opportunities, and questions that are common to a journey through grief as I have experienced and observed it. They cover such topics as *anger, guilt, the duration of grief, heartache, tears, humor, depression, insomnia, asking for help, bad days, loss of status, dealing with memories, negative feelings, facing pain, self-nurturing, letting go, feeling abandoned, and God's presence*. Grieving, however, is not a linear journey. There is no uniform response to loss, and there is no predictable order or pace for grieving a loss. While there are common stages of grief, each person grieves in a unique manner. Accordingly, these reflections are meant to be open-ended, allowing each reader to provide content and conclusions that are appropriate to individual situations.

These reflections are intended to be used in the way that is most helpful to the reader. They can be read **selectively**, depending on what topic matches a particular situation, in their **entirety** as a non-linear journey through the grieving process, or in some combination. They can also be used as a resource for **individual daily meditations**. Each reflection contains a portion of a psalm, a response to the psalm, and a short prayer or repetition from the same psalm. Readers may want to respond to the psalm from their own experience before reading the entire reflection. For those who would like a broader scriptural context for daily meditations, I have provided companion Old and New Testament reading references at the end of each reflection, based on the Lectionary of the Episcopal *Book of Common Prayer*.

Most of the translations of the psalms used in this book are taken from *The New Revised Standard Version*. Exceptions are Psalms 23, 78, 90, 116, 139 (*King James Version*) and Psalms 56, 85, 143 (*Book of Common Prayer*). Readers may want to consult their own personal choices for translations of the psalms.

My hope is that these reflections will provide a source of support, comfort, and encouragement to those who are living through loss.

STEPS

Psalm 37   *Though we stumble, we shall not fall headlong.*

One of the games we played for hours in the backyard of my childhood home was "Mother, May I?" To make moves in the game, we asked permission of the leader to take a specified number of different kinds of steps—baby steps, giant steps, frog leaps. My favorite was scissor-cut steps, which required a high leap while clicking your feet together in the air. Not all of the steps were forward. We frequently took steps sideways, backwards, and diagonally.

The object of the game was to be the first one to get to the leader, and of course the leader controlled that movement by giving permission. But whoever succeeded was leader for the next game and got to control the outcome.

It is something like that in grieving—we attempt to move forward to the point where we have more control of our circumstances, rather than the circumstances dictating to us how we are feeling and doing. As in the game, grieving is a series of steps, many small ones—and not all of them are in a forward direction.

Our steps are made firm by the Lord...though we stumble, we shall not fall headlong, for the Lord holds us by the hand.

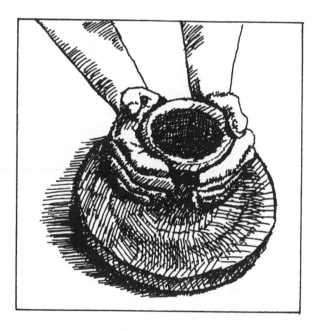

MEMORIES

Psalm 100 *Make a joyful noise to the Lord, all the earth. Worship the Lord with gladness; come into his presence with singing.*

Easter Sunday is a triumphant service, filled with festival music and great rejoicing. My church is decorated for Easter with magnificent white banners and Easter lilies. People arrive for the service early with a sense of excitement and anticipation that is unique to Easter Sunday. The morning begins with the raising of the Alleluias which the children had buried in our church's garden at the start of Lent. We sing familiar hymns, loudly and enthusiastically. The mood is one of overriding joy.

This Easter I was singing loudly and participating joyfully when I remembered something that made me sad. After my brother and I left for college, our parents attended the early service every Easter Sunday, then drove eighty miles to the nearest city so they could eat Easter dinner in their favorite cafeteria, where my father could have turkey and my mother lamb. Later in the day they would call to wish me a happy Easter and to say how they had spent the day, which was always the same. As I sat in church, I wanted very, very much for my parents to have one of those Easter Sundays, which ended with my father's death ten years ago. This memory and my tears lasted the remainder of Easter service.

In a sense, grieving never ends. We will always have memories that make us sad, and sometimes they blindside us. But I believe in those memories—sometimes painful and sometimes joyful—as reflective of the valuable relationship that I grieve.

For the Lord is good; his steadfast love endures forever, and his faithfulness to all generations.

Additional Daily Readings: Isaiah 49:1–7; Matthew 12:14–21

BUTTONING MY BUTTONS

Psalm 131 *My soul is like the weaned child that is with me.*

Sarah lost more than a spouse when her husband died. She lost her best friend, her lover, her confidant, and her favorite traveling companion. She also lost her plumber, accountant, dish washer, grocery shopper, financial consultant, wood stacker, and fellow gardener. What hurt even more, however, was that she had no one to button her buttons.

Sarah went through the grieving process like a good soldier, doing all the right things. She cried copiously, attended a grief support group, and talked openly about her loss. Sarah did grief work in abundance, and experienced all the stages of grief, moving back and forth through them toward a new life. She relied on her friends, deepened relationships, hired a plumber, took on new professional and volunteer responsibilities, learned how to prepare her taxes and manage her financial affairs, had the wood delivered and stacked, and gradually found satisfaction working alone in her garden.

After all of that progress, Sarah still had no one to button her buttons. Along with this lingering sadness, however, she can now read her husband's love letters and look at his pictures with quiet joy.

But I have calmed and quieted my soul, like a weaned child with its mother; my soul is like the weaned child that is with me.

Additional Daily Readings: Numbers 23:11–26; Matthew 22:1–14

SELF-NURTURING

Psalm 4 *You gave me room when I was in distress.*

When we are in distress, we cannot always depend upon outside support at exactly the right time or in exactly the right way to meet our needs of the moment. Others either may not be available to us or if they are, may do or say something that is not helpful. So when we are feeling most needy and dependent—in distress—we may find ourselves all alone.

What does the psalmist mean by "gave me room when I was in distress"? What is the room for?

When we are in that aloneness, perhaps it is the time and space to *nurture ourselves*, to do something special "just for me." Nurturing ourselves could take the form of an outward activity such as going for a walk in a favorite environment, taking a bubble bath, eating a special meal, reading a book, sipping a cup of tea; or it could be how we talk to ourselves on the inside, saying something especially kind.

The Lord gives me "room when I am in distress." How do I use it?

Be gracious to me, and hear my prayer.

Additional Daily Readings: Daniel 1:1–21; John 17:1–11

Reflected Light

Psalm 50 *The Mighty One, God the Lord, speaks and summons the earth from the rising of the sun to its setting.*

When I take an evening walk, I enjoy looking at the night sky, always unpredictable. Last night was clear, cold, and cloudless. As I began my walk, I glimpsed the full moon, rising between a pine and a cedar tree. Whether it was the result of weather conditions, my imagination or the state of my spirit, a full moon had never looked as big and round and bright to me. I followed the moon all through the neighborhood and around a park loop. The moon only seemed to grow larger and brighter as it rose.

This morning, I walked back to the park and looked at the morning moon, the same moon I had watched the night before. While smaller and more subdued than last night, it was still numinous.

God shines forth in our lives, in expected and unexpected ways. Sometimes it is reflected light.

Out of Zion, the perfection of beauty, God shines forth.

Additional Daily Readings: Zechariah 14:4–9; Luke 21:25–31

Release

Psalm 33 *Praise the Lord with the lyre; make melody to him with the harp of ten strings.*

Last night, in the span of less than an hour, I experienced what felt like the entire process of grieving as I listened to a young pianist play a Rachmaninoff piano concerto with our local symphony orchestra.

There was a shock at the beginning as I sensed an emotional intensity for which I was unprepared. As the performance continued, I found myself intermittently sighing and smiling and crying, and I had momentary rushes of anger that I was letting myself be overwhelmed by the memories of grief at an event that should have been an escape. I felt a deeply depressed melancholy as I listened—unsure whether it was the composer's or the pianist's or my own. The music leaped forward, then backed up in small steps to pick up echoes from earlier sections of the piece. The music moved on but not in a systematic way: two steps forward, one step back, then forward again, but always honoring the memories.

At the end I felt uplifted, as tears streamed down my cheeks, and I stood to applaud the pianist and the orchestra, and I felt strengthened by something outside of myself to go back out into the world.

Sing to him a new song; play skillfully on the strings, with loud shouts.

Additional Daily Readings: Genesis 12:1–8; John 3:1–17

BAD DAYS

Psalm 68   *Blessed be the Lord, who daily bears us up.*

I am having a bad day. Last night I had trouble going to sleep, I was awake and restless during the night, I woke up too early, and now I feel tired and listless. My head and heart are filled with sadness. Nothing comforts me. The one new thing I tried recently ended in failure. I feel distant and disconnected from my friends. I feel desolate. Nothing ahead in my day seems appealing. Nor will anything help.

Then I am hard on myself. "You shouldn't feel this way; feeling sorry for yourself isn't going to help either. You are indulging in self-pity. Think of something positive. Do something positive." But I do not have the desire or energy to get moving, to get on with my life this day.

So finally I tell myself maybe it's all right to feel sad and "off" some of the time. Maybe I should just let myself have this bad day. And enjoy it.

God gives the desolate a home to live in.

Additional Daily Readings: 1 Samuel 12:19–24; Acts 16:16–34

ANGER

Psalm 103 *He will not always accuse, nor will he keep his anger forever.*

We are angry. We have lost someone or something important. A husband, in the prime of his life, broadsided by three drunk teenagers. An only child, in an automobile accident. A young son, from a brain tumor. Both parents in the same year. A spouse and a family unit, from divorce. A wife, before she could enjoy her grandchildren. A long-established business. A mother, from a slow and painful cancer death. The dog who was always there, loving unconditionally.

All of these losses have been suffered by members of a support group dealing with loss. I read that anger is one of the stages of grief. I understand that anger is a normal response to an important loss, no matter what the cause. But reading or hearing that doesn't make the anger go away.

It does help to know that I have companions on my journey. It does help to know that God is merciful, even if I do not always know how or when.

The Lord is merciful and gracious, slow to anger and abounding in steadfast love.

Additional Daily Readings: Joel 2:1–2, 12–17; Matthew 6:1–6, 16–21

TRYING SOMETHING NEW

Psalm 110 *From the womb of the morning, like dew, your youth will come to you.*

"What is the one thing you would tell someone who is experiencing what you went through?" I asked my friend Patti, who was emerging from a long period of grief after the sudden death of her husband. She said, "I would tell them *don't be afraid to try something new. Sometimes it works, and sometimes it doesn't, but don't be afraid to try.*"

In my youth and young adulthood, trying new things was easy. I knew I would succeed. As I have gotten older, however, I have found myself increasingly resistant to change. Now I know the risks. And I know what it is like to experience failure. Considering new things stirs up a lot of inner argument about why I shouldn't.

But I also know the positives that can result from trying new things. What I need is that feeling of confidence I had in my youth to balance the knowledge and experience of middle age—from the womb of the morning, like dew.

He will drink from the stream by the path; therefore he will lift up his head.

Additional Daily Readings: Zechariah 2:10–13; John 3:31–36

A Steep Descent

Psalm 26 *Prove me, O Lord, and try me; test my heart and mind.*

One of the paths I regularly hike begins with an extremely steep climb. There are some parts of the ascent with switchbacks and some parts where the trail is just straight up. After the steep part, the trail levels off and winds through thick foliage, across a small stream, and through banks of wildflowers in the spring and summer. Whatever the season, the landscape smells good, and I feel rich when I am on that trail.

When it is time to go home, I have to climb back down the steep place where I began. Every time I start on the hike I am relieved when I get to the top, the level place on the trail, because I think I have done the hard part, and going down will be easier. But it never is. The steepness hurts my knees, and my toes burn from bumping against the ends of my hiking boots on the descent. There is one place that is so steep and slick that I have to sit down and slide on my backside.

Why, I ask myself, every time, is it harder to go down than up? Is the Lord testing my heart and mind?

For your steadfast love is before my eyes, and I walk in faithfulness to you.

Additional Daily Readings: Isaiah 5:13–17; Luke 21:29–38

Fear Not

Psalm 55 *Fear and trembling come upon me, and horror overwhelms me.*

Mack's hands trembled and his feet wouldn't move. Afflicted with tremors and rigidity of movement, the ultimate diagnosis of Parkinson's Disease left Mack, in middle age, retired on disability due to the severity of his symptoms. Faced with a choice of how to spend the rest of his life, Mack decided to find some positive things to do, even if he will have to do them eventually from a wheelchair.

He is actively involved with the Habitat organization in our community as a board member and volunteer office manager. Drawing on his professional experience in the printing business, he has helped establish a graphics communication course to train prisoners so that they will have a job skill when released from prison, substantially reducing the recidivism rate for those who complete the course. Mack also coordinates the lay readers in our parish.

With his mysterious talent for involving others in his projects, Mack formed a support group for persons with Parkinson's and other chronic diseases. The group named itself the "Movers and Shakers." Among the group members who meet weekly for lunch, there is much laughter and teasing and enthusiasm for life. There is considerable trembling, but little fear.

But I will trust in you.

**Additional Daily Readings: Isaiah 35:1–10;
Matthew 11:2–11**

HAS GOD FORGOTTEN ME?

Psalm 77 *My soul refuses to be comforted.... Has God forgotten to be gracious?*

Because of greater-than-normal snowfalls during the winter, heavy spring run-offs and flooding are expected in mountainous regions this year. Emergency teams are training to deal with potential problems from flooding, including rescuing people from rising waters and flooded areas.

Yesterday I watched one of the emergency teams practicing flood rescue techniques. They were learning to navigate through rising, swirling waters in small rescue crafts. One man practiced maintaining a position in these waters. That's all he did. He paddled harder and harder in the rapids in order to stay exactly where he was. The more he worked, the less he moved.

Forward movement can be tough. Sometimes the harder I work, the less I move. And I don't even have to practice.

At times like that I wonder where God is.

Your way was through the sea, your path, through the mighty waters; yet your footprints were unseen.

Additional Daily Readings: Genesis 25:19–34; John 7:37–52

CLEANSING GROWTH

Psalm 1 *They are like trees planted by streams of water, which yield their fruit in its season.*

Across the back of my property, the previous owners had planted a row of photenia shrubs. Some were healthy, producing a beautiful green leaf tinted with copper, and some had no foliage at all. On the advice of a gardening friend, I tried watering the unhealthy ones profusely, but that did not seem to help. Nothing else, such as putting mulch around them, seemed to help either. All of the healthy ones continued to thrive, and all of the unhealthy ones continued to wither.

One Saturday afternoon in a fit of anger at my teenage daughter, I marched out to the tool shed and dramatically selected the largest clippers in the shed. I hacked and whacked off all of the dead growth, every brown leaf and every drooping branch. I hacked and whacked until all that was left of the unhealthy shrubs were stumps and leafless branches. In the process, I hacked and whacked off all of my anger at my daughter.

In addition to releasing the anger, another positive outcome emerged several days later: I noticed new growth emerging from the hacked and whacked photenia bushes.

And their leaves do not wither.

**Additional Daily Readings: Ezekiel 37:1–10;
Romans 8:18–27**

A Child's Insight

Psalm 8 *Out of the mouths of babes and infants.*

A literal question about death asked by a child can sometimes lead to the deepest level of spiritual insight.

Jake, the husband of my friend Bernice, died recently after a long illness. At the funeral service, the minister talked about Jake and how he was going to live with Jesus in heaven. Among the family members attending the funeral service and the burial was Vanessa May, Bernice's five-year-old granddaughter.

After the service, family and friends gathered at Bernice's home to eat, drink, celebrate, grieve, and share remembrances of Jake.

In the midst of the sharing, Vanessa May got into Bernice's lap. She asked, "How is Paw-Paw going to get to heaven? Is Jesus going to come down and get Paw-Paw out of that hole?"

Bernice, wiping tears from her cheeks, began to laugh her special laugh that rumbles out from somewhere deep inside her body and causes her entire body to shake. Then she nodded.

What are human beings that you are mindful of them, mortals that you care for them?

Additional Daily Readings: Exodus 34:1–8; Luke 2:15–21

Senseless Loss

Psalm 10 *Their eyes stealthily watch for the helpless; they lurk in secret like a lion in its covert.*

One of the families in my neighborhood built a beautiful outdoor scene for Christmas. There was a nativity set with the baby Jesus, Mary, Joseph, shepherds, and wise men, all lit with colorful lights above a manger. Beside the scene, they put a large Christmas card that read, "Peace on earth, good will towards men."

A friend and I walked by the scene each night and were distressed to discover that pieces of the nativity were being systematically stolen. First the shepherds went. The family put in their place a sign, "Shepherds stolen on December 9." Then two of the wise men went, and that night there was a sign, "Two wise men stolen on December 10." The next day the other wise man was gone. Then Mary and Joseph. And finally, the baby Jesus.

We visited our neighbor to see if we could help in any way. He said the police suspected students from our university, but they have had no success in finding them or the missing objects. He also said he was having trouble explaining what was happening to his nine-year-old daughter.

All that was left in the outdoor scene was the empty manger and the sign, "Peace on earth, good will towards men."

His hand is stretched out still. (Isaiah 9:17)

Additional Daily Readings: Isaiah 9:8–17; Mark 1:1–8

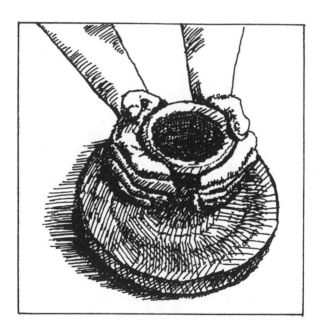

Finding Comfort

Psalm 23 *Yea, though I walk through the valley of the shadow of death, I will fear no evil: for thou art with me; thy rod and thy staff they comfort me.*

Five years ago Debbye's son committed suicide. He was nearing the completion of his senior year in high school. She and her husband returned from a meeting one evening and found him dead, having shot himself in the closet of his bedroom. Not only was Debbye faced with the sudden death of her son, but she also had to deal with the social stigma attached to a death from suicide. Her burden has been heavy.

Recently in church our congregation read together Psalm 23 as the psalm appointed for that Sunday. I talked to Debbye after the service. She said that this psalm has been an ongoing source of comfort to her. Sometimes it has been her sole source of comfort. Debbye believes that she and her son shared this psalm during a eucharist following his death.

It is not uncommon for persons who have suffered the loss of a loved one, particularly when the death is sudden or traumatic, to experience the presence of that person after the death. Many describe the experience as the return of their loved one to say good-bye, something that they did not have an opportunity to do.

While we each have our own reasons, Debbye and

many others of us find comfort in the words of Psalm twenty-three.

He restoreth my soul.

Additional Daily Readings: Nehemiah 9:6–15; John 10:1–10

FOULING UP

Psalm 78 *They did not keep God's covenant, but refused to walk according to his law; they forgot what he had done, and the miracles that he had shown them.*

Peter is one of my favorite characters in the Bible because he does very human things, like forgetting the wonders the Lord has shown him. When Peter shows up in the gospels, I always breathe a sigh of relief. Peter is genuinely well-meaning, but he always fouls up.

He promises the Lord, "I am ready to go with you to prison and death." After Jesus is betrayed by Judas and taken away, Peter follows at a distance. A woman sees Peter and says he was with Jesus, but Peter denies it. A little later someone else says that Peter is "one of them," but Peter says, "I am not." After an hour, still another person insists that Peter was with Jesus, and Peter says, "Man, I do not know what you are saying." Sure enough, the cock crows.

I am relieved when Peter shows up because I can count on his fouling up. And when he fouls up, that lets me off the hook.

Doesn't it?

They tested God again and again.

Additional Daily Readings: Isaiah 8:1–15; Luke 22:31–38

GRACE

Psalm 92 *Those who are planted in the house of the Lord shall flourish.*

We don't always know what to expect when we plant a seed. In the mail, I received a gift packet of Blue Lake green bean seeds. Although it was already late fall, and the only place I had to plant the seeds was in a bed that was not very sunny, I planted the seeds. While I was putting them into the ground, my neighbor came from across the street. A professor of plant physiology, he asked with great interest what I was doing, and I told him I was planting Blue Lake green beans. He looked at my packet, assured me I was using top quality seeds, then kindly suggested that spring or early summer might be a better time to plant these seeds, and also I might consider a sunnier location. All of this exchange occurred in a good-neighborly spirit.

Defying conventional gardening expectations, the beans flourished—producing abundantly. When I learned that my neighbor's family of twenty-three was in town for a holiday meal, I took him a gift of one Blue Lake green bean with a festive bow. He and his wife laughed until they had tears running down their cheeks. His wife said she was going to steam the bean and divide it into twenty-three servings.

God's grace appears in the house of the Lord, in unsunny bean beds, and in other unexpected places.

How great are your works, O Lord!

Additional Daily Readings: Jeremiah 7:1–7, Luke 6:39–49

NEGATIVE FEELINGS

Psalm 109 *May his children wander about and beg; may they be driven out of the ruins they inhabit. May the creditor seize all that he has; may strangers plunder the fruits of his toil. May there be no one to do him a kindness.*

Portions of the psalms are repellent. There are many sections which have as their themes judgment, vindication, resentment, hatred, brutality, and cruelty. The images are specific and vivid. There are psalms that I can hardly read without cringing. There are psalms that I can hardly read at all.

Perhaps for different reasons, there are aspects of life and of dealing with loss—my own and others—which cause me to recoil. I have thoughts and feelings that are so dark and negative that I wouldn't want anyone to know about them.

The psalms are not all sweetness and light; they are filled with dark images. They describe a wide range and deep intensity of negative emotions. They meet us where we are.

We can skip over the hard parts or we can own them as part of us, as part of what we are experiencing: very negative feelings.

My heart is pierced within me.

Additional Daily Readings: Ezekiel 11:14–25; Luke 10:17–24

BIRTHING

Psalm 139 *You knit me together in my mother's womb.*

Pregnancy and grieving may appear to be opposite processes—the one dealing with birth and the other dealing with death or loss. We think of pregnancy as a time of joyous expectation, grieving as a time of deep sadness. Yet they may have much in common.

Pregnancy, like grieving, results in dramatic changes—physically, emotionally, and spiritually. Everything is different. Biorhythms are affected, causing disruptions in sleeping and eating habits. Energy levels are affected. There are volatile mood swings, like an emotional roller coaster; and often there are dream language and dream images that are altogether new. Both are times that require making special efforts to take care of one's self: eating healthily, exercising regularly, getting enough rest. And both are times of serious spiritual stock-taking. There is a period of intense pain.

After nine months of nurture in the mother's womb, a child is born. After a process of inner growth that occurs during grieving, a new self emerges.

I praise you, for I am fearfully and wonderfully made.

Additional Daily Readings: Isaiah 61:1–3; Luke 11:9–13

LETTING GO

Psalm 46 *Be still, and know that I am God!*

One summer Sunday I was sitting in church, sitting still as a matter of fact, half listening to the sermon and half reviewing my plans for the upcoming week. My ears heard, "Be still, and know that I am God," from the sermon, while my mind raced forward with a variety of possible schedules to accomplish my personal and professional objectives.

Then I made the mistake of listening to more from the sermon: "In Hebrew, one of the words used for 'be still' is 'Raphah,' which means 'to let go.'"

I knew Psalm 46 well, and I never heard anything like that. Being still just meant to be quiet, not to move around. Like in prayer or meditation. God never said anything about letting go of anything. What did I need to let go of? That's a lot to ask, I thought. Letting go of something. Or some things.

What do I need to let go of in my life? What will happen if I am still?

Be still, and know that I am God!

Additional Daily Readings: Isaiah 28:14–22; Luke 13:22–30

GIVING

Psalm 20 *May he remember all your offerings.*

We had a miracle in our parish the Friday before Thanksgiving. Our food pantry is open Friday mornings from 10 until 12, and we had made an effort within the parish to have turkeys available that morning. Word got around the community we serve that we were giving away turkeys, and sixty-seven individuals or families had come by shortly before noon. Prior to the opening of the food pantry we had collected exactly sixty-seven turkeys to give away. But that wasn't the miracle. At 11:50 two more families arrived for their turkeys. The people running the food pantry were about to tell them there were no more, when a parishioner arrived bearing two turkeys. That was the miracle: sixty-nine people needing turkeys, and sixty-nine turkeys available to share.

We cheered when we heard the story in church the following Sunday. I cheered loudly, but I also cheered guiltily. My contribution to the turkey distribution was coupons from one of the local grocery stores; for each twenty-five dollars I spent, I received one "turkey buck." With ten "turkey bucks," the store gave away a free turkey. I contributed five turkey bucks to pool with other parishioners' turkey bucks.

I know how to contribute from my abundance; I would

like to learn how to give from all of the living that I have.

Some take pride in chariots, and some in horses, but our pride is in the the name of the Lord.

Additional Daily Readings: Deuteronomy 26:1–11; John 6:26–35

SHELTER

Psalm 27 *For he will hide me in his shelter in the day of trouble; he will conceal me under the cover of his tent.*

Where do we seek shelter in times of trouble?

One weekend I went on a camping trip in the mountains of New Mexico with some companions. We set up a tent for shelter and sleeping. For the evening meal we grilled steaks, which we planned to eat around the camp fire while looking at the evening stars. Just as the steaks were done, we heard thunder, followed about five minutes later by the beginning of a rain storm which turned into a deluge.

We hurriedly moved into the tent with our plates of food. It was dark in the tent, but dry and safe. I cut into my steak with enthusiasm, so much enthusiasm that I cut all the way through the meat, the paper plate, and the floor of the tent. Before I could finish my first bite, water was pouring into the tent from the hole in the floor.

I do not know of any human-made place that is consistently safe in time of trouble.

And I will offer in his tent sacrifices with shouts of joy; I will sing and make melody to the Lord.

Additional Daily Readings: Genesis 15:1–12, 17–18; Luke 13:22–35

FINDING OUR VOICE

Psalm 84 *My heart and my flesh sing for joy to the living God.*

The image of flesh "singing" brings to mind some of the livelier rehearsals of my hometown church's junior choir in which I participated as a pre-teen. Whenever we could manage it, my friend Ann and I sat next to one another in the middle of the three choir pews. That way, we were surrounded by other choir members, and the choir director Mrs. Disworth couldn't see what we were doing.

Mrs. Disworth had a soprano voice that quavered when she sang high notes. This quavering caused Ann and me to giggle, uncontrollably, and our giggling made the pew shake. Even if one of us could manage to stop, the shaking pew was enough to start the other one of us giggling again. I don't know how many verses of "There's a Wideness in God's Mercy" and "Fairest Lord Jesus" we sang while giggling and shaking. I do recall that Mrs. Disworth frequently moved Ann or me to the front pew during most choir rehearsals.

My memories of growing up in the church and singing in the junior choir are joyful ones. In the front of my *Book of Common Prayer*, I still carry a photograph from our local paper of the 1952 St. Phillip's Episcopal Church Junior Choir. Ann and I are smiling in the first row.

Happy are those who live in your house, ever singing your praise.

Additional Daily Readings: Jeremiah 31:7–14; Matthew 2:13–15, 19–23

GOD'S MERCY

Psalm 85 *Show us your mercy, O Lord.*

Betty entered the Hospice program when her illness became terminal. She and her family were told by the physician that she would die soon—within days or at best, a few weeks—and the death might be messy, from hemorrhaging. But Betty looked and acted healthy. She continued to eat well; her husband Buddy made her biscuits every morning for breakfast and anything else she wanted during the day. She confounded everyone by not dying right away. Weekend after weekend, relatives came to say goodbye, and some came several times. The family celebrated Easter and the birthdays of two grandchildren, with Betty participating fully.

She always seemed positive and centered, yet was not in denial about her condition. I spent a considerable amount of time with her, and I was amazed that I always left feeling energized. I asked her once if she did anything in particular to stay centered and she said, "No, I don't say any special prayers or anything. I just feel close to God."

One morning before breakfast Betty fell asleep in the living room. Buddy offered her breakfast, but she couldn't wake up. With the help of a Hospice aide, Buddy moved her back to the bed they had shared every night for forty-nine years and eleven months. Family members gathered and kept watch through the day as she slept. Buddy made more biscuits. Betty died peacefully in her sleep shortly before midnight.

God shows mercy in *God's* own way.

Mercy and truth have met together.

Additional Daily Readings: Jeremiah 10:11–24; John 8:21–32

STRUGGLING

Psalm 95 *For he is our God, and we are the people of his pasture, and the sheep of his hand.*

A sheep shearer's work is hot, hard, and mesmerizing. The shearer picks a sheep, grabs the hind leg, and drags the wriggling animal toward the shearing machine. He throws the sheep and begins with the legs, then works the underside. The wool comes off in thick strips, like carpet samples, exposing the sheep's tender skin in ever-widening amounts as the shearer steadily works the animal's body. After completing the underside, the shearer straps the animal's legs together and does the sides and back, while the sheep struggles against the clippers.

When all the wool is shorn, the shearer releases the animal to go bleatingly into the heat, free of its heavy coat. The sheep appears wobbly and disoriented at first, then steadies as it finds balance and freedom. The shearer grabs another hind leg without breaking rhythm.

Sometimes I struggle against the Lord's spirit, just as the sheep struggles against the man's clippers. I am wobbly and disoriented. With the Lord's spirit working actively in my life, I find balance and freedom.

O that today you would listen to his voice!

Additional Daily Readings: Ezekiel 34:11–17; Matthew 25:31–46

AMBIVALENCE

Psalm 104 *People go out to their work and to their labor until the evening.*

A man whose wife died after a lengthy illness went to the grocery store several days after her funeral. It was hard for him to believe that people were just going about their ordinary business of shopping for groceries. They were going about the ordinary business of their lives: working, talking, eating, shopping.

How could they do that, he wondered, when his wife had just died? Didn't they know how he felt? He wanted to tell them, he wanted them to comfort him. At the same time he didn't want to tell them, he wanted to be left alone. But he still didn't see how they could just go around the store shopping for groceries—not knowing.

C. S. Lewis wrote after the death of his wife in *A Grief Observed*, "There is a sort of invisible blanket between the world and me. I find it hard to take in what anyone says. Or perhaps, hard to want to take it in. It is so uninteresting."

You cover it with the deep as with a garment.

Additional Daily Readings: Job 38:1–11, 16–18; Luke 12:13–21

GUILT

Psalm 5 *Make them bear the guilt, O God.*

Grief work can be fraught with "if onlys." If only I hadn't let my son take the car that night. If only I had stayed at the hospital another hour. If only I had worked on improving the relationship before it was too late. If only I hadn't let my cat go outside. If only I had told my father I loved him. If only it had been me instead of him. If only I had done or if only I hadn't done....

Dealing with guilt is an ongoing struggle in grief. We may be able to accept on an intellectual level that there is nothing we can do about "it" now, and that there is no point in feeling guilty. But getting that message through to our hearts and memories is more challenging. Much more.

It might help to think about what we would tell others who are feeling guilty in grief. Or what we would tell someone else who is in an identical situation to our own. And then to listen to what we would say.

Give ear to my words, O Lord.

Additional Daily Readings: Genesis 3:1–24; John 1:19–28

PARADOXES

Psalm 10 *Why, O Lord, do you stand far off? Why do you hide yourself in times of trouble?*

In this psalm, as in many others, God is both far off and near, both present and absent. How can that be?

A place that I love to ride my bicycle is a path that winds through a long, narrow valley with towering mountains on either side. Though it is a strenuous route, I feel comfortable and secure pedaling along this protected mountain-encased path.

On one afternoon's ride, a couple of miles from home, I was caught in a sudden blowing rain storm for which I was unprepared. The rain peppered against my face and body so hard that it hurt, and the day darkened frighteningly as ominous clouds rolled in. I was cold, wet, and scared. As there was no good place to seek shelter, I decided to press on for home. I rode as fast as I could against the wind, and I lowered my head for protection and speed.

Occasionally I would look up to see where I was going and to assess my progress. Whenever I raised my head, I could see light at the end of the valley ahead of me.

But you do see! Indeed you note trouble and grief, that you may take it into your hands.

Additional Daily Readings: Ruth 1:19–2:13; Luke 13:10–17

How Long?

Psalm 13 *How long must I bear pain in my soul, and have sorrow in my heart all day long?*

How long will I grieve? How long will I hurt? Everyone grieves in their own way, at their own pace. And grief depends upon the circumstances of the loss: whom you have lost, what the relationship was, how the loss occurred. Grief also depends on the circumstances of one's own life when the loss occurred. Still, it would help to know when I will feel better.

No two losses are the same, so no two people's recovery times are the same. The death of a child is different from the death of an adult. Loss of a spouse is different from loss of a parent. Losing a pet is different from losing a family member. A lingering death is different from sudden death. Loss from divorce is different from loss from death. Loss of one's home from fire is different from loss of one's home from a move. What's certain is that the loss you are suffering now is the one that is most intense for you.

The memories never go away, nor would we want them to. But gradually, the pain will lessen; our bodies and spirits will heal. Grieving takes hard work and time. How much time? As much as *you* need.

How long, O Lord?

Additional Daily Readings: Amos 3:1–11; Matthew 21:12–22

Repetitions

Psalm 18 *The Lord is my rock, my fortress, and my deliverer, my God, my rock in whom I take refuge, my shield, and the horn of my salvation, my stronghold.*

In this one verse, the image of the Lord as a source of strength and protection is repeated over and over again. The psalms frequently contain such repetitions. Psalmists find many different ways in a single psalm to present the same ideas, feelings, and images.

While grieving is a process in which an individual moves toward regaining balance in life, it is not a linear process. We go forward a few steps, and then we go back. Just when we think we are leaping ahead, we may find ourselves moving sideways or backwards or turned upside down. We may feel confident and in control one day, depressed and desperate the next.

Hearing the same thing again, especially something that has helped in an earlier part of the process, can sometimes help get us unstuck. The repetitions pull us back into the journey to wholeness.

The Lord is my rock, my fortress, and my deliverer, my God, my rock in whom I take refuge, my shield, and the horn of my salvation, my stronghold.

Additional Daily Readings: Isaiah 12:1–6; John 7:37–52

Your Heart's Desire

Psalm 20 *May he grant you your heart's desire, and fulfill all your plans.*

The leader of a support group in which I participate gave us each a single sheet of plain white paper and told us to split the sheet in half. On the first half we wrote down something we wanted to give up. After everyone had written that down, we were instructed to tear up what we had written. The leader collected all of our scraps and threw them in the wastebasket.

On the other half of the sheet, we wrote down something we wanted to add to our lives. This half was more difficult for me. There was something I had been thinking about wanting to have happen in my professional life, but I had not articulated it to anyone, even fully to myself. Still, that's what I honestly wanted, so I wrote down my desire somewhat timidly, hoping that no one would see it. The leader then told us to pass our papers to the persons on our left and on our right so they could sign and date our declarations as witnesses. Now everyone will know my secret, I thought. But the persons on my left and right signed without reading what I had written, just as I did with theirs.

Relieved, I asked cheerfully, "Does this guarantee we're going to get what we've asked for?"

The leader said, "That depends upon you, doesn't it?"

Now I know that the Lord will help.

Additional Daily Readings: Daniel 3:19–30; Luke 4:1–13

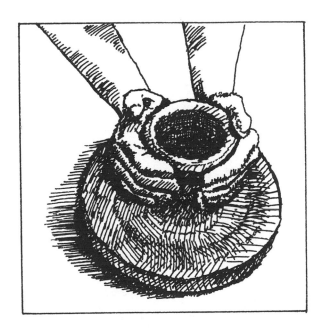

FEELING OF ABANDONMENT

Psalm 22 *My God, my God, why have you forsaken me?*

It was Good Friday afternoon and Sam, age four, was at the park with his mother after they had spent some time at the church helping with the food pantry and apparently discussing the day's theology. About one o'clock Sam asked, "Is Jesus dead yet?" His mother looked at her watch and said matter-of-factly, "No, not until three o'clock." Sam then asked, "Is it summer yet?" And his mother said, "No, not yet, it's still spring, and summer comes after spring." Then he asked, "Does fall come after summer?" and his mother said, "Yes, fall comes after summer." And Sam asked, "Can I go play on the slide?" and his mother said, "Yes, but be careful." A few minutes later Sam came back and asked, "Is Jesus dead yet?" His mother looked at her watch and said, "No, not for about another hour."

Attempting to understand things in his life, Sam sometimes asks questions that are profound. He sometimes asks questions about things that are difficult or impossible to explain and understand. Yet he would like an answer. According to today's reading from Matthew, "About three o'clock Jesus cried with a loud voice, 'Eli, Eli, la'ma sabach-tha'ni?' that is, 'My God, my God, why have you forsaken me?' "

O my God, I cry by day, but you do not answer; and by

night, but find no rest...future generations will be told about the Lord, and proclaim his deliverance to a people yet unborn.

Additional Daily Readings: Isaiah 52:13–53:12; Matthew 27:1–54

GOD'S TABLE

Psalm 23 *Thou preparest a table for me in the presence
of mine enemies; thou anointest my head with oil; my
cup runneth over. Surely goodness and mercy shall
follow me all the days of my life; and I will dwell in the
house of the Lord for ever.*

Sherry and her teenage daughter Elsa joined our
parish about a year ago. At first, only Sherry came to
church. After she became comfortable with the service
and got to know some of the parishioners, Sherry began
to bring Elsa to Sunday services. Elsa is mentally
retarded. She walks awkwardly, her hands and head
move jerkily, and her speech is difficult to understand.

The procedure for holy eucharist in our church is for
communicants to form two lines in the center aisle and
move forward to receive communion at a semi-circular
altar. Fr. Jeff, the priest, administers the bread, and lay
chalice bearers administer the wine. Sherry brings Elsa
through the line and as they near the altar, Elsa sometimes stops, frightened and uncertain about going forward. When this happens, Fr. Jeff stops distributing
bread and beckons to Elsa. He smiles and waves her
forward, and she moves slowly and clumsily toward the
altar. When she gets close enough, Fr. Jeff hugs her
warmly. Sometimes they talk to each other, and sometimes they just embrace.

Then he continues the process of the holy eucharist,

giving out bread—to Elsa and to Sherry, and to others at the altar.

This is my body, which is given for you. Do this in remembrance of me.

Additional Daily Readings: Isaiah 7:10–25; Luke 22:14–30

EXPECTATIONS

Psalm 26 *For your steadfast love is before my eyes, and I walk in faithfulness to you.*

A friend and I traveled to the Lost Maples State Natural Area in west Texas to view the bigtooth maple trees. Descendants of eastern sugar stock maples that migrated west during the Ice Age, they are an anomalous sight in this barren landscape. The maples survive only in rare sheltered canyon pockets, like this park. Having looked at many photographs of their impressive fall foliage display, I was eagerly anticipating actually seeing the trees.

After a stop at the park's information center, we set out enthusiastically with our map to walk along the "maples trail." Soon, we found the maples—magnificent but leafless. We had somehow failed to consider the state of a maple's foliage in late winter.

Somewhat disappointed, we decided to continue our walk and at least get some good exercise. We hiked by a creek through narrow canyon walls, along a path that smelled richly of the cedar trees that lined the way, then up a steep trail that traversed open grasslands, scrub oak, and madrone. We climbed and climbed, through juniper, ash, and black cherry, as we listened to the distant calls of canyon wrens. Finally, we came to an overlook which had one of the most spectacular views I have ever encountered. We could see the Sabinal River hundreds of feet below; a clear blue sky above; and across the horizon, all the way to yonder.

I went to the area expecting to see maple leaves, and I left with a vision of something else.

O Lord, I love the house in which you dwell, and the places where your glory abides.

Additional Daily Readings: Jeremiah 31:15–17; Matthew 2:13–18

SPEAKING TO GOD

Psalm 29 *The voice of the Lord is powerful.... The voice of the Lord breaks the cedars.... The voice of the Lord shakes the wilderness.... The voice of the Lord causes the oaks to whirl, and strips the forest bare.*

The voice of the Lord is powerful, so powerful that it can break trees, shake the wilderness, and strip a forest.

But what kind of power do our human voices have? Although it sometimes feels like not very much, the scriptures contain evidence that our voices can be imminently powerful when speaking to God, that is when we are truly *speaking to God*.

In the Old Testament, for example, Jonah speaks to God from the belly of a great fish, of all places. After fleeing his mission as a prophet and being thrown into the sea by sailors, Jonah is swallowed by a fish. He calls to the Lord in his distress, and the Lord hears Jonah's voice—from inside this fish in the depths of the sea. And the Lord responds by speaking to the fish, which spews Jonah out upon the dry land.

Jonah's voice was powerful enough to be heard from the belly of a fish. How do we speak to God?

May the Lord give strength to his people!

Additional Daily Readings: Jonah 2:2–9; John 11:17–27, 38–44

BELIEVING IN YOURSELF

Psalm 32 *I will instruct you and teach you the way you should go.*

My friend Babe is infinitely creative in dealing with the obstacles she encounters. On a recent summer afternoon, Babe and I went into the mountains for a picnic lunch, where we sat beside the mighty waters of a creek which Babe wanted to brave.

I worried because the waters were moving dangerously fast, and I was afraid that Babe would be swept away among the treacherous rocks. But she walked beside the creek, patiently, looking for just the right place. When she found it, Babe jumped into the water.

Dog Babe had selected a narrow place in the creek, a place where the width of the creek bed just matched the length of her body. She securely tucked herself into that space, wedging her front and back paws against either bank. Head up, Babe relished the roaring waters as they splashed against the dam she had created with her body.

With a firm belief in her objective and her self, Babe relies on instinct and intelligence to solve seemingly insurmountable problems, large and small.

At a time of distress, the rush of mighty waters shall not reach them. You are a hiding place for me; you preserve me from trouble; you surround me with glad cries of deliverance.

Tasting

Psalm 34 *Oh taste and see that the Lord is good.*

The best part of my childhood summers was visiting my grandparents for two weeks all by myself. During those visits, my grandmother would fix me anything I wanted to eat. My favorite meal—well before the days of counting cholesterol and fat grams—was fried chicken, mashed potatoes, cream gravy, buttermilk biscuits, real butter, corn on the cob, and fresh green beans which I would help pick from my grandfather's garden. While I was helping my grandmother in the kitchen, my grandfather would come in to "check" the corn, which involved holding my arm, pretending to put butter and salt on it, then nibbling up and down my arm and pronouncing the corn "just right." For dessert, the neighbors would bring over a freezer of homemade peach ice cream which we would eat out back on the red tiled patio with my grandmother's freshly baked pound cake, still warm from the oven.

Just before bedtime, I climbed into my grandmother's lap in her recliner, and we planned the next day's meals and the parts I could help her cook. Every morning my grandfather took me to the cafe on the courthouse square for a doughnut and Dr. Pepper and a visit with his friends.

I savor the taste and memory of those meals, snacks, and the unconditional love that came with them.

I am the bread of life.

**Additional Daily Readings: Deuteronomy 8:2–3;
John 6:47–58**

How We Wait

Psalm 40 *I waited patiently for the Lord.*

For me, the appropriate words to the psalm would be I waited *im*patiently for the Lord. Or I waited in frustration or I waited impetuously or I waited in anguish. Waiting patiently is not something I do well.

But sometimes we have to wait. There are processes that cannot be rushed. There are circumstances over which we have no control. Dealing with loss takes time—a lot of it. And there is no way to predict how long grieving will last. It may be months or years. Each individual is different, and each loss is different.

How we wait can affect the quality of our life experience in every moment of the process. *How* we wait can affect the outcome.

I waited patiently for the Lord; he inclined to me and heard my cry. He drew me up from the desolate pit, out of the miry bog, and set my feet upon a rock, making my steps secure.

Additional Daily Readings: 1 Samuel 31:1–13; Mark 5:21–43

DON'T APOLOGIZE

Psalm 42 *Why are you cast down, O my soul, and why are you disquieted within me?... Why must I walk about mournfully?*

Walking around mournfully demands no apology or explanation. It is a healing necessity for anyone who has lost someone or something important. Mourning is a normal response to the abnormal event of loss, and we mourn the loss in order to honor its importance: spouse, child, parent, friend, pet, home, marriage, job, way of life. Whatever the loss, it is our loss and it matters.

Mourning provides a period of transition from the time the loss occurs through whatever time it takes to acknowledge the sadness and to integrate the differences in our lives and our selves that the loss has effected. This time helps us get to a place where we can allow the memories in without being overwhelmed by pain, where we can claim our circumstances and find new meaning for our lives.

Because of its importance, some cultures provide prescribed rituals for mourning that include modes of behavior and apparel. In some ways that would make it easier—but most of us are pretty much on our own to work out these things. Or are we?

My tears have been my food day and night.... These things I remember, as I pour out my soul: how I went

*with the throng, and led them in procession to the house
of God, with glad shouts and songs of thanksgiving.*

**Additional Daily Readings: 2 Kings 5:1–15; Mark
1:40–45**

WHAT IS MY WEALTH?

Psalm 52 *"See the man who would not take refuge in God, but trusted in abundant riches, and sought refuge in his wealth!"*

On a regular basis I spend a considerable amount of time on "my wealth." I review my bank checking account, read the financial statements I receive in the mail on investment and retirement funds, take care of necessary tax records, and make decisions relating to financial matters. I love to watch my wealth accumulating, during the periods when it does, and I worry when movement seems to be in the opposite direction.

I have never thought about how much wealth is "enough." I just know that it is important to have more than I do now. And more after that.

Something else I've never thought about is what it would be like to seek refuge in God rather than in my wealth. Maybe I do not even know what my wealth is.

But I am like a green olive tree in the house of God.

Additional Daily Readings: 1 Samuel 24:1–22; Mark 4:1–20

Tears

Psalm 56 *You have...put my tears into your bottle; are they not recorded in your book?*

Tears are a healthy part of living with loss. In spite of what some in our culture would have us believe, tears are evidence *not of weakness* but *of healing*. It is important to find ways of releasing our feelings of sadness, and crying helps us do that.

Some researchers who have studied the tears of grieving believe that they are different from the tears of joy and may contain chemicals that relieve stress in the body. Studies indicate that tears of sadness release substances that actually have a calming effect.

It is obvious to the psalmist that God recognizes the value of tears. They are so important that God collects the tears in a bottle and records them!

In God I trust; I am not afraid.

Additional Daily Readings: Ecclesiastes 7:1–14; Matthew 15:21–28

SITTING STILL

Psalm 62 *For God alone my soul waits in silence.*

Two pieces of advice frequently given to persons dealing with loss are to allow yourself time to be still and to spend some time helping others. Following one of these pieces of advice taught me an important lesson about the other.

My friend Katy is struggling to lose weight. She has been off and on diets for several years. They help for a while, but Katy eventually finds an excuse to return to former habits. Still, she tries because she wants to and the excess weight is contributing to other health problems. Katy said that one of the difficulties she has is that she rushes around in the ebb and flow of daily life and doesn't take time to prepare healthy meals for herself. Instead, she will eat something hurriedly on the run and use that as her excuse not to eat sensibly. Katy came up with the idea of a symbol that would help her: an egg timer. She said the egg timer would remind her to slow down and think about what she was eating, as she watched the sand flow through the funnel.

Eager to be a supportive friend—"helping others"—I rushed out and bought us both egg timers, Katy's to help her with her weight and mine to remind me to think of Katy.

When I used the egg timer, I found that I could not sit still long enough for the sand to flow from top to bottom.

For God alone my soul waits in silence, for my hope is from him.

Additional Daily Readings: Isaiah 49:8–18; Matthew 6:24–34

THIRSTING

Psalm 63 *My soul thirsts for you.*

What does it mean for a soul to thirst for God?

I know what it means for my body to thirst. I ran in a 10K race on a hot and humid day. Having done this distance in similar conditions, I knew to drink before the race and at regular intervals along the course. But due to some sort of breakdown in communications and planning, there was no water at the aid stations. None. I stopped at every one, and there was nothing to drink. All of the containers had been emptied by runners ahead of me. When I got to the 6K marker, I felt desperate, but I didn't want to quit. I kept running, knowing there must be water at 8K. But there was none. In all of my life, I can never remember being so thirsty. I completed the race in a daze.

During that run I had a glimmer of understanding about what it might mean for my soul to thirst for God. I was so thirsty for water that I thought of nothing else.

O God, you are my God, I seek you; my soul thirsts for you...as in a dry and weary land where there is no water.

Additional Daily Readings: Deuteronomy 11:1–12; Matthew 13:44–58

WATER INTO WINE

Psalm 65 *The pastures of the wilderness overflow, the hills gird themselves with joy, the meadows clothe themselves with flocks.*

And it is happening before my eyes—it is spring in the mountains, and the fields are blanketed by the season's first wildflowers, dandelions and crocuses. In the pastures there are flocks of newborn baby lambs with their mothers. Skipping through the fields, the hills and I gird ourselves with nature's joy—all of which inspired a new adventure: making dandelion wine.

Having no experience in this art, I sought the tutelage of a friend who had made many a season's batch. We picked the dandelions, brought them home, washed them, carefully picked out the blossoms, and put them into a large jar. We added boiling water, sugar, orange juice and peel, raisins, and later yeast and honey water—all in mysterious portions specified by my friend. We stirred up the mixutre and put a lid on the jar, leaving a small opening for venting.

Then I said, "I'm ready to try it." My friend said, "No, it will take a while to ferment." "How long?" I asked. "A day? A week? A month?" My friend said, "A while."

Now I'm waiting. Daily, I stir the mixture; I strain it; I smell and observe changes, as the liquid turns a golden yellow and the composition does unknown things. As much as I like to control outcomes, this one is beyond me.

For a while.

You visit the earth and water it, you greatly enrich it; the river of God is full of water; you provide the people with grain, for so you have prepared it.

Additional Daily Readings: Deuteronomy 8:11–20; John 2:1–12

LISTENING

Psalm 66 *But truly God has listened; he has given heed to the words of my prayer.*

How do we know that God hears our prayers?

Patti lost her husband in the prime of his life. Her grief was deep and long-lasting, reflecting the quality of the deep and loving relationship she had with him.

On a vacation in Colorado, two years after his death, she took a long walk along an isolated mountain stream and sat down on a rock next to the stream. The day was still and quiet. As she watched the water flow, Patti prayed to God to somehow let her feel the closeness of her husband. Surprised to hear the rustling of leaves, she looked up. Gently, along the creek bed, the aspens began to quake in the distance and then the quaking moved closer and closer to where she sat, as if the wind were carrying the movement of the leaves toward her. She sensed the presence of her husband, coming with the quaking of the leaves.

Patti marks that moment as a significant turning point for the better in her grieving process. And rustling aspens continue to remind her that God listens.

Blessed be God, because he has not rejected my prayer or removed his steadfast love from me.

Additional Daily Readings: Exodus 12:14–27; Mark 16:1–8

VISION

Psalm 67 *That your way may be known upon earth.*

Sister Bernadette called from the Monastery of St. Clare to tell me she had just been diagnosed with pancreatic cancer, and the end was very near. As usual, she sounded upbeat and cheerful. When I went over to visit with her, we had a wonderful conversation about life and death, interspersed with her duties of running the monastery and answering telephone calls about an upcoming auction of miniature horses, which the monastery breeds and sells to support its main business of contemplative prayer.

She said she believed her dying process was another aspect of her witness to faith, just as her life had been. I asked Sister Bernadette if she had a vision of life after death. She said she didn't have any concrete vision but she had a sense of what it would be like, drawing on her experiences of contemplation in which she felt God's presence as a physical force, inhabiting her entire being: a moment of perfect peace.

She also said she hoped she wouldn't look down and worry about how things were going at the monastery.

May God be gracious to us and bless us and make his face to shine upon us.

Additional Daily Readings: Isaiah 49:5–13; Matthew 28:16–20

Does Anyone Understand?

Psalm 69 *I sink in deep mire, where there is no foothold; I have come into deep waters, and the flood sweeps over me. I am weary with my crying; my throat is parched. My eyes grow dim with waiting for my God.*

Frequently I say or am tempted to say to someone else, "I know how you are feeling." But probably I don't know. Even when that person is experiencing something I have been through or is in a situation similar to one I am in currently, I doubt that I know how they are feeling. I can empathize, but I cannot know.

Does anyone know?

There are moments when I am sure that the psalmists who wrote many hundreds of years ago understand how I am feeling. And not only do they know, but they represent my feelings to God. Openly and honestly, without pretense.

I do not have to do anything but let them speak.

Save me, O God, for the waters have come up to my neck.

Additional Daily Readings: Isaiah 50:4–9a; Matthew 26:1–5, 14–25

ASKING FOR HELP

Psalm 70   *But I am poor and needy; hasten to me, O God! You are my help and my deliverer.*

It is hard to admit being needy, whatever the cause. It feels like defeat, like giving up. We learn to put up a brave front, to be strong, to hide our neediness. For many of us, just admitting we need help is very difficult. Asking for help is even harder.

When we have suffered a loss, we are needy. We hurt. We hurt inside and out. Although what we need during the grieving process will be different for each of us and will vary depending upon where we are in our own grieving process, we all need to express our feelings. We need to tell our stories, sometimes again and again. We need to admit we are hurting. Crying is not a sign of weakness, it is a sign of healing.

We can ask for help from family members, from friends, from support groups, and from professional counselors. We can also ask for help from God, right now, on the spot—and any time of the day or night.

O Lord, do not delay!

Additional Daily Readings: Jeremiah 4:9–10, 19–28; John 5:19–29

COURAGE

Psalm 71 *Do not cast me off in the time of old age; do not forsake me when my strength is spent.... You who have made me see many troubles and calamities will revive me again.*

As a free-lance writer, much of what I receive in the mail is rejection. Some of these rejections are personal letters that say my work is well-written but not quite right for that particular publication. Some of the letters are addressed to me personally but seem to have been written by a computer and reflect no real consideration of what I have submitted. The worst blow of all is when I receive a form letter addressed to "Dear Contributor" or "Dear Writer" and signed by "The Editors." Or not signed at all.

What's interesting to me is that I almost never receive a rejection when I'm having a good day or a good period in my writing—when I am in shape to handle rejection. Instead, they seem to come when I am already down about something else. When my self-esteem is really low, I receive one of the form letters to "Dear Contributor" about the one piece of work that came from the best heart and spirit of my writing.

Is there ever a good time to suffer a loss? Why does it happen to people in old age, when strength is spent? Why does it happen in the prime of our lives? Why does it happen when we are already down?

I pray for the courage to send my work out again one more time.

From the depths of the earth you will bring me up again.

Additional Daily Readings: Jeremiah 1:4–10; Luke 4:21–32

Sleeplessness

Psalm 77 *In the night my hand is stretched out without wearying; my soul refuses to be comforted…. You keep my eyelids from closing.*

Grieving is wearying. But when I most need my strength, I cannot sleep. I wake up in the middle of the night, wide awake, and stay awake the rest of the night. Or I have trouble falling asleep. Or I doze and wake many times during the night. When I get out of bed in the morning I feel exhausted, which makes it even harder to get through the day.

During these episodes of wakefulness, I tell myself, "You *must* go to sleep. You need you rest. *Go* to sleep. *Now*." Such admonitions, of course, only aggravate the problem.

Is there a solution? People in my grief support group try different things: reading the telephone book, listening to a meditation tape, drinking herbal tea, listening to music, cleaning the house. Those who are well along in the grieving process say it gets better—they now have periods of sleeping through the night.

It is my grief that the right hand of the Most High has changed.

Additional Daily Readings: Isaiah 58:1–12; Mark 9:30–41

SHIELDS

Psalm 84 *For the Lord God is a sun and shield.*

We all wear shields to protect ourselves. Our shields come in different forms and sizes and depths. Sometimes our shield is a mask to hide behind because we can be safe only if people do not know who we really are, what we are really like. Wearing the mask enables us to function efficiently and effectively in the work place, in social situations, at home and even with those to whom we feel closest. The mask keeps us safe because we don't reveal our true selves.

Sometimes our shields take the form of protection for our feelings and emotions. Without it, we might let others know how we feel and risk getting hurt by their reaction or indifference. Sometimes that same shield covers our needs. If we admit what we need, we run the risk of being disappointed that our needs won't be met.

What if we didn't wear the shields? What if we took the risks? What if we let God be both sun and shield?

Happy are those whose strength is in you.

Additional Daily Readings: Isaiah 2:1–5; Matthew 24:37–44

RE-CREATION

Psalm 87   *Singers and dancers alike say, "All my springs are in you."*

On an especially memorable Christmas, I received a pogo stick as a gift. It was black and white striped, with a plastic horse's head to hang onto, and a wonderful spring. I spent all of Christmas Day on that pogo stick, beginning by bouncing up and down our driveway. Then I braved the sidewalk. I rode my stick all the way down the block and back, many times, past all the neighbors, waving and jumping, being joined by other children in the neighborhood who had also received Christmas pogo sticks.

I felt free in a way that I had never experienced: the sensation of being able to go higher and higher, farther and farther, with no known limit.

I bounced until dark and after; I continued hopping until my parents told me it was time to come inside. But the next morning I was out again early with my pogo stick, springing into the sunrise.

On that Christmas morning many years ago, I had newborn springs. Is it possible to re-create them?

All my springs are in you.

Additional Daily Readings: Joshua 3:14–4:7; John 9:1–12, 35–38

TOOTHBRUSHES, PUMPS, AND FAITHFULNESS

Psalm 89 *Steadfast love and faithfulness go before you.*

When we suffer a serious loss, we go through a process of grieving to deal with that loss. The grief that we feel is a measure of the quality of the relationship that we have lost. People grieve in different ways, at their own pace; there is no right or wrong way to get through it.

One man I know whose wife died almost a year ago has been able to sort through and deal with all of her belongings except her toothbrush. "I just can't bring myself to move her toothbrush," he says, "so it is still in the rack next to mine." Another friend has a ceremony each year on the anniversary of her son's death; family and friends gather and talk about her son, to cry, to remember, and to laugh. Some cannot yet look at photographs; others are sustained by them. Some eat all the time, and others lose their appetites. One friend was embarrassed, then amused, to find herself wearing one blue pump and one brown one to church several weeks after her husband's death.

Even though the stories are hard to hear, and it makes me sad to know that others are suffering, I find comfort in hearing the stories of others who are grieving, and I find comfort in telling my own—in listening and being heard. These sharings of intimate personal experiences and caring sustain me in living through loss.

I find faithfulness all around me.

Your faithfulness surrounds you.

Additional Daily Readings: Isaiah 42:1–9; Acts 10:34–38

SUDDEN LOSS

Psalm 90   *The days of our years are threescore years and ten; and if by reason of strength they be fourscore years....*

For some, the span is much less than seventy or eighty years. Those who experience the sudden death of a loved one know with tragic certainty how quickly a life can be snatched away.

A friend's husband smelled gas and went out to their tool shed to locate the problem. When he opened the door, there was an explosion. He burned to death, and my friend suffered severe burns herself in the unsuccessful effort to save him. She was in the intensive care unit of the hospital during his funeral, and is still dealing with severe burn wounds as well as her deep, deep grief. In an instant, she lost her husband, her home, and her own health. She weeps from pain, pain on the inside and pain on the outside.

Her tears are part of her grieving and part of her journey to healing and wholeness. Her tears are also a reminder that each day is a gift.

So teach us to number our days, that we may apply our hearts unto wisdom.

Additional Daily Readings: Amos 5:6–7, 10–15; Mark 10:17–27

AGING

Psalm 92 *In old age they still produce fruit; they are always green and full of sap.*

My next-door neighbor, a widower, is about eighty something. He is an elegant gentleman, with a serene countenance, snow-white hair, a lean build, and graceful movements.

He spends much of his time working in the yard, setting out new plants and clearing away old ones, watering and weeding, putting out bird seed in his feeders. When not working, he watches. He can hardly wait to get up in the morning to watch his flowers bloom and his ornamental beans grow up the trellis and the birds feed and the seasons change. He also watches the unfolding mysteries in his backyard pond, which he has developed as a completely self-contained ecological system.

And he is a generous neighbor, frequently passing along an "extra" flat of plants or an "extra" bird feeder.

I see the hand of God each day when I look at my neighbor and the natural beauty that surrounds him. In old age, he produces an abundance of good fruit.

For you, O Lord, have made me glad by your work; at the works of your hands I sing for joy.

Additional Daily Readings: Exodus 33:18–23; John 21:19b–24

CONSOLATIONS

Psalm 94 *When the cares of my heart are many, your consolations cheer my soul.*

In a troubled mood, I went to church one Sunday morning with many cares on my mind, none of them spiritual. Two of my friends in the congregation are Sandra and her pre-school son, Charles. We don't always see each other on Sundays because we attend different services, but when we overlap, Charles always gives me a big hug. If we haven't seen each other for several Sundays, Charles gives me several hugs to make up for the Sundays we have missed.

On this particular morning, I saw my friends as I entered the sanctuary. I had arrived just as the church was quieting down for the service to begin. Sandra and Charles were on their way out. When the sanctuary became completely silent, Charles announced loudly to his mother (and everyone else in the congregation), "I *have* to give Lyn her hugs," which he did.

Thank you, God, that when the cares of my heart are many, you send consolations to cheer my soul.

When I thought, "My foot is slipping," your steadfast love, O Lord, held me up.

Additional Daily Readings: Lamentations 1:17–22; Mark 11:27–33

LONELINESS

Psalm 102 *I lie awake; I am like a lonely bird on the housetop.*

After an especially difficult, desolate, and lonely night—with long periods of sleeplessness, during which I am sure I lay awake and groaned—I opened my blinds in the early morning light and looked out at my bird feeder. Sitting on top, preparing to go in for food, was one little chickadee. Before the chickadee could eat, a large male cardinal arrived and scared the smaller bird away. The cardinal occupied the feeder and continued to hold off the chickadee.

The chickadee approached, retreated, approached, and retreated, fluttering at the entry like a humming-bird. Finally, it braved the feeder and entered. Much to my surprise—and I suspect that of the little chickadee—there were no problems. Pretty soon another chickadee approached and joined the other two birds, then another. One male cardinal and three little chickadees ate peacefully together at my bird feeder. I learned something important from watching the birds about getting along with others even though we are different.

And I no longer felt alone.

Hear my prayer, O Lord; let my cry come to you. Do not hide your face from me in the day of my distress.

Additional Daily Readings: Jeremiah 23:1–8; John 6:52–59

Sweaty Spirits

Psalm 103   *Bless the Lord, O my soul, and all that is within me, bless his holy name.*

Several years ago I made a covenant with a good friend to memorize some of our favorite prayers, hymns, psalms, sections of psalms, and verses from scripture. We agreed to memorize one selection each week for a six-month period. Unfortunately, she chose Psalm 103 in its entirety as one of the selections we would memorize.

Whew! The language that inspired my friend to choose Psalm 103 also makes it tough to memorize. And that psalm is much longer than anything else we worked on. I finally figured my best hope was to do a short section each day during my morning exercise. I divided the psalm into seven sections and copied each section on an index card. In the morning when I was out running or walking, I would work on that section and keep the previous sections in my pocket for review. By the end of the week, the first few days' cards were unreadable from sweat. Whenever I encounter Psalm 103, I still see the verses on sweat-drenched index cards.

But I made it. And the end is easy because it is exactly like the beginning: Bless the Lord, O my soul.

Bless the Lord, all his works, in all places of his dominion. Bless the Lord, O my soul.

THROUGH THE DESERT

Psalm 105 *He opened the rock, and water gushed out.*

There have been times in my life when I felt that things just could not continue the way they were going. I needed change, and I wanted something dramatic to happen to help me make that change. When I feel like that, I pray—in desperation. A miracle would be desirable, but even a sign would suffice. I expect God to open the rock and for water to gush out.

It never happens that way. Not once has God opened a rock for water to gush out. I look everywhere for it, but I have never found water gushing out of rock that God has opened in response to my plea.

But several days or weeks or months later, I look back on that time and remember. A friend said something kind. Something positive developed in my work life. I saw a brilliant sunset. My teenage daughter suggested we do something together. I made an important decision and acted on it. I participated in an exciting community project. My students were enthusiastic about a new idea. Someone wrote me a special note.

God opened a rock and the water gushed out. It flowed through the desert like a river.

They asked, and he brought quails, and gave them food from heaven in abundance. He opened the rock, and water gushed out; it flowed through the desert like a river.

Additional Daily Readings: Daniel 6:1–15; Luke 5:12–26

Heartache

Psalm 109 *For I am poor and needy, and my heart is pierced within me.*

Many people who are grieving describe not only a "pierced" heart but heartache as a very real physical pain. Some say it feels like a heavy weight pressing on their chests; others describe it as a sharp pain, as if a knife had pierced the heart; and others say it feels like an intermittent shooting pain, throbbing from inside. Although these physical symptoms, including heartache, are quite common in grief, they are scary to the person who is suffering from them.

In discussing reactions to loss, I frequently hear the comment, "Oh, that happened to you too? I thought I was crazy." Sharing with others doesn't necessarily make the heartache go away, but it does relieve some of the contributing anxiety to know that what you are experiencing has happened to others in grief—and they have survived.

With my mouth I will give great thanks to the Lord; I will praise him in the midst of the throng.

Additional Daily Readings: Jeremiah 18:1–11; John 6:27–40

SPEAKING OF ONE WHO HAS DIED

Psalm 115 *They have mouths, but do not speak...they make no sounds in their throats.*

We sometimes find it difficult to talk to someone who is grieving about the person who has died. Perhaps we fear we will say something wrong or say something that will make them feel worse. In some cases, the hardest thing of all is to say the dead person's name—out loud. Yet the person who has suffered the loss needs opportunities to talk about the loved one and possibly about the circumstances surrounding the loss.

I was making a bereavement call on Brent, who had lost his wife Dolly; the same day I had read an article in the paper about people's reluctance to talk about someone's loss for fear of opening old wounds, but the importance of bringing the loved one's name into normal conversation to allow the grieving person opportunities to speak of the loss. Determined, I brought up Dolly's name as early as I could in the conversation. Before I could say anything else, even finish my sentence, I burst into tears. Brent looked at me and got tears in his eyes.

We changed the subject to fishing for a while, and then we talked about Dolly and what she had meant to our lives.

The Lord has been mindful of us; he will bless us...
both small and great.

Additional Daily Readings: Exodus 12:40–51;
Matthew 28:1–16

BEING BROUGHT LOW

Psalm 116 *I was brought low.*

Being brought low, however it occurs and whatever the cause, is a humbling experience. A very humbling experience. Just ask Artie.

As the only male creature among the cats and dog in my household, Artie has something to prove. He likes his own space, he likes to show the other creatures who's tough, and he likes to show off.

Combining all of these objectives, he set out one morning to climb a tree in the back yard. The other animals looked on enviously from outside the house and the humans watched interestedly from inside the house. Artie easily clawed his way up ten feet past several branches to his favorite limb. Then he strutted—not walked but strutted—out to the end of the limb. Just as he was about to look down with his best "lording it over you" glance, Artie slipped and fell off the branch.

He scattered leaves while plummeting through the short branches on his descent, trying unsuccessfully to grab a foothold and his dignity. He hit the ground with a loud thump. It took several seconds before Artie could move, and when he finally did, he moved very slowly.

Gathering himself as best he could Artie walked—not strutted but walked—away from the tree and sought refuge under the picnic table. It took a lot of courage for Artie to pass by the other animals.

I was brought low, and he helped me…. Thou hast delivered my soul from death, mine eyes from tears, and my feet from falling.

Additional Daily Readings: Isaiah 43:1–12; Luke 24:13–35

GIFT OF EACH DAY

Psalm 118 *This is the day that the Lord has made; let us rejoice and be glad in it.*

Many years ago, I developed symptoms that indicated the possibility of a life-threatening disease. After extensive tests and considerable anxiety, the diagnosis was something far less serious than the doctor and I feared. In relief and thanksgiving I vowed that I would begin each day with the verse from this psalm: *This is the day that the Lord has made; let us rejoice and be glad in it.*

There are mornings when I wake up full of energy and excitement about what is ahead in my day, and there are other mornings when I wake up and can hardly open my eyes, much less leap out of bed with enthusiasm. Some mornings I feel sad or I awake filled with worry and anxiety. Other mornings I feel positive and centered.

What remains a constant through my waking moods is honoring that promise that I made many years ago. Hard as it sometimes is, I remind myself that the Lord has given me this day, a day that I might not have had; this day is for rejoicing and gladness.

This is the day that the Lord has made; let us rejoice and be glad in it.

Additional Daily Readings: Genesis 8:6–16; John 20:11–18

Serving Others

Psalm 119:121–144 *I am your servant; give me understanding.*

Web, now retired from a full-time job, volunteers her time freely to support various activities in her local community, including her church, the Hospice organization, the public library, the local hospital, Meals on Wheels, a local historical society, and the Head Start Program. As Web gives of herself to others with grace, compassion, and understanding, she is truly a servant of the Lord.

And Web tells some very interesting stories about how she comes to understand the Lord's testimonies in her role as servant. One morning she arrived freshly groomed and eager to begin her volunteer time with a new Head Start class. Before reading the day's story, she gathered the children around her in a circle and said, "I always want you to feel free to ask me about anything. Would any of you like to ask a question before we begin?"

Lucinda, the smallest girl in the class, raised her hand.

Web said sweetly, "Lucinda. Do you have a question?"

Lucinda asked, "Why do you wear lipstick on your teeth?"

Your decrees are wonderful; therefore my soul keeps

them. The unfolding of your words gives light; it imparts understanding to the simple.

Additional Daily Readings: Jeremiah 18:1–11; John 6:27–40

God's Presence

Psalm 121 *I lift up my eyes to the hills.*

The country where I live is flat. Since there is nothing in the natural landscape above eye level, I can lift up my eyes to the hills only in a metaphorical sense.

As much as I love my home terrain, I also enjoy spending time whenever possible in the Colorado Rockies. When I am in that part of the country, I literally have to lift up my eyes to see the mountains that surround me. Whatever is happening in my life—internally and externally—is altered by that perspective. I am always awed by their majestic, transcending presence. The normal things in my life, especially the problems, seem less important but somehow clearer in that landscape. I feel *overpowered*, and at the same time, *empowered*.

As I watch the light change across their surfaces, as I smell the pines and summer wildflowers, as I breathe and taste the clear air, as I listen to the sound of a mountain stream and feel its cold water on my bare toes, I am intensely aware of the presence of God—who made those mountains so that I could lift up my eyes and know.

My help comes from the Lord, who made heaven and earth.

CHANGE IN STATUS

Psalm 123 *We have had more than enough contempt. Our soul has had more than its fill of the scorn of those who are at ease.*

Carol, recently widowed, went to the bank to open a checking account. Over the years, she and her husband had opened many such accounts in various locations and had always been treated with respect and courtesy. Carol told the receptionist she wanted to open an account and was referred to a "new accounts" clerk who asked, without any greeting, for her social security number and identification, then disappeared.

Meanwhile, at the next desk, a middle-aged couple arrived to open a new account, were greeted warmly by another "new accounts" clerk and began their process. While Carol waited, they completed their account-opening and left the bank. When Carol's clerk finally returned, he looked at a computer printout, said her credit was ok, and that she could open the account. Carol realized she had been treated differently, including a credit-check, for no apparent reason. She left the bank feeling humiliated.

Many times since her husband's death—with acquaintances, at restaurants, at business establishments, in social gatherings—Carol has been aware that the loss of her husband changes her "status" in the minds of some. Although cruel and unfair, it is something Carol must deal with on a regular basis.

Again and again Carol reminds herself that she is a *person*, deserving of respect and fair treatment. And that she is not alone.

So our eyes look to the Lord our God, until he has mercy on us.

Additional Daily Readings: Judges 18:1–15; Acts 8:1–13

Laughter and a Celebration Casserole

Psalm 126 *Then our mouth was filled with laughter, and our tongue with shouts of joy.*

Like tears, laughter has a major part in grief work. Laughter is a great stress reliever, and it helps release some of the pain we carry around inside of ourselves after suffering a loss.

My Uncle Clinton helped me financially through college and supported me in intangible ways through many other critical stages of my life. He was always there for me. When he died, I was heartbroken. I knew I had lost a person for whom there was no replacement.

After the funeral, the family gathered in his apartment to eat dinner, and many friends had brought in food. We decided on a menu for the evening which included a delicious-looking squash casserole. I was responsible for cooking the squash casserole, and I put it in the oven at 350 degrees for thirty minutes. We all served our plates and sat down to eat. People began to giggle, and when I took a bite of the squash casserole, I realized why. It was literally ice cold; I had somehow neglected to notice that it was frozen when I put it in the oven. The giggles turned to hilarious laughter, which continued throughout the rest of the meal—after I recooked the casserole in the microwave.

When I think of my Uncle Clinton, I remember our special relationship, and I remember eating frozen squash casserole in celebration of his death and life.

Those who go out weeping, bearing the seed for sowing, shall come home with shouts of joy, carrying their sheaves.

Additional Daily Readings: Ruth 1:15–22; Matthew 5:13–20

Uttermost Darkness

Psalm 139 *If I take the wings of the morning and dwell in the uttermost parts of the sea, even there shall thy hand lead me, and thy right hand shall hold me.*

When I hear these words of Psalm 139, I think about my friend Julia. As a child, she held baptismal services for her dolls at the family's dining table, using her mother's best cream pitcher as the baptismal font. She always preached a sermon afterwards, with the salt and pepper shakers listening intently in the congregation. Now middle-aged, Julia was recently ordained to the priesthood with her parents, husband, three children, and many friends present to celebrate.

Some time between childhood and middle age, Julia and I were talking about our favorite psalms. She said she liked Psalm 139 because she could not think of a darker place to dwell than in the uttermost parts of the sea. "And even in that darkest place," she said, "even in the uttermost parts of the sea, God is there to lead us and to hold us. I find that very comforting."

So do I.

The night shineth as the day; the darkness and the light are both alike to thee.

Additional Daily Readings: Isaiah 61:1–9; Matthew 5:1–12

FINDING A PATH

Psalm 143 *Let me hear of your loving-kindness in the morning, for I put my trust in you; show me the road that I must walk, for I lift up my soul to you.*

Sharon tried again and again to begin exercising as part of a program to develop a healthier lifestyle. She was successful in reducing fat in her diet and in other aspects of the program, but she just could not make herself exercise regularly. Sharon started and stopped a variety of exercises—walking, swimming, water aerobics, dry land aerobics—with groups and on her own.

Nothing worked. After a few weeks she would find an excuse to stop. Getting to a health club was inconvenient. She preferred walking, but she didn't have time before work, and after work she was too tired; there wasn't a suitable place because she lived in the country, and there were loose dogs on the road to her house.

Many months ago Sharon read Psalm 143 as part of her daily meditation. She decided to use verse eight as a morning prayer: "Let me hear of your loving-kindness in the morning, for I put my trust in you; show me the road that I must walk, for I lift up my soul to you." Then she asked her husband to mow a path around a large pasture beside their home.

Since then, Sharon has maintained a regular walking program around her pasture. Sometimes she picks dewberries.

Teach me to do what pleases you, for you are my God; let your good Spirit lead me on level ground.

Additional Daily Readings: Job 2:1–13; John 6:27–40

HOW MANY STARS?

Psalm 147 *He heals the brokenhearted, and binds up their wounds. He determines the number of the stars.*

One of my treasured childhood memories is sitting with family and friends around a camp fire beside the Frio River. After hamburgers, hot dogs, and at least two kinds of cake, we sang songs and waited for the dark. When it got dark, we roasted marshmallows, watched the blinking light of fireflies reflecting on the river, and took turns telling scary ghost stories.

Then we looked up at the stars. I am convinced that those Frio River camp fires were under more stars than I have ever seen in any evening sky. Sometimes I would lie on my back, look up, and try to count the stars. I never counted them all, and no one else did either. We always gave up at several hundred. Or several thousand.

It is an enormous comfort to know, as the psalmist says, that God will heal us when we are brokenhearted and will bind up our wounds. What I find even more amazing, though, is that God knows how many stars are up there in that evening sky.

Great is our Lord, and abundant in power; his understanding is beyond measure.

Additional Daily Readings: Isaiah 61:10–62:3; John 1:1–18

SAINTS

Psalm 149 *Praise the Lord! Sing to the Lord a new song.*

Due to a childhood illness, I spent a week confined to bed. The illness occurred while I was visiting my maternal grandparents, and the duty of caring for and entertaining me fell to my grandmother. An active churchwoman, my grandmother suggested that we spend some of our time together with her teaching me the words to hymns. She would sing the line, and I would sing it after her, then we would add another, and another, until I could do the entire verse, and eventually the entire hymn.

We may have worked on others, but the one I remember to this day is, "I Sing a Song of the Saints of God." I was confused about the line, "and I mean, God helping, to be one *too*," because I thought I was singing...to be one *two*, which didn't make a lot of sense, but at least it was easy to learn since I was good at numbers.

The line that made the greatest impact, however, was the one that goes: "You can meet them in school, or in lanes, or at sea, in church, or in trains, or in shops, or at tea."

I asked my grandmother, "You mean, I might meet a saint anywhere?" and she said, "Yes."

You can meet them in school, or in lanes, or at sea, in

111

church, or in trains, or in shops, or at tea, for the saints of God are just folk like me, and I mean to be one too.

Additional Daily Readings: Ecclesiasticus 44:1–10, 13–14; Matthew 5:1–12

LEGACY

Psalm 78 *For he established a testimony...which he
commanded our fathers, that they should make them
known to their children; that the generation to come
might know them.*

Every person leaves a legacy. When someone we love
dies, we are responsible for keeping that legacy alive
and passing it along to future generations.

My father loved to ride around the small west Texas
town where we lived, and I loved to go with him. We
would talk about everything that was happening in our
community, and he would point out any new develop-
ments.

During these outings, we would always stop for pie
and coffee at one of the gathering places in my hometown. Our favorite was the Kincaid Hotel. We would
visit with all the people in the coffee shop, and then we
would sit down to have our pie and coffee—which for me
was a soft drink. My father would give me his cream,
which came in little glass milk bottles, and I would
drink it right out of the little bottle.

Just before we left the cafe, my father would always
say, "Now *this* is the romance of the living business."

*That the generation to come might know them, even
the children which should be born; who should arise
and declare them to their children.*

Bright Orange Hair

Psalm 96 *Oh sing to the Lord a new song.*

Mary and Pete's bedroom had always been blue—blue walls, blue ceilings, blue curtains, blue bedspread. For the fifty-two years of their marriage, the bedroom was blue, their favorite color. A few months after Pete's death, Mary had the bedroom painted yellow, and she bought bright orange accessories: bright orange curtains and a bright orange bedspread. To top it off, she had her hair dyed to match the curtains and bedspread.

Her children, relatives, and friends were appalled. They whispered among themselves. "What's the matter with her? When is she going to be her old self again?"

When is Mary going to be her old self again? The answer is *never*. She may let her hair go to grey again, but Mary will never be the same.

Loss changes us. Permanently. We are shocked, numb, scared, angry, sad, depressed, guilty, restless, withdrawn, self-pitying, accepting, and ultimately *different*. Each small step in recovery brings some relief, even though a reminder may come up and start the pain all over again. As we discover new resources—from within and without—we sing a new song. Perhaps in bright orange hair.

Oh sing to the Lord a new song; sing to the Lord, all the earth.